AF269748

LIGHTNING BOLT BOOKS™

Strong Submarines

Marie-Therese Miller

Lerner Publications ◆ Minneapolis

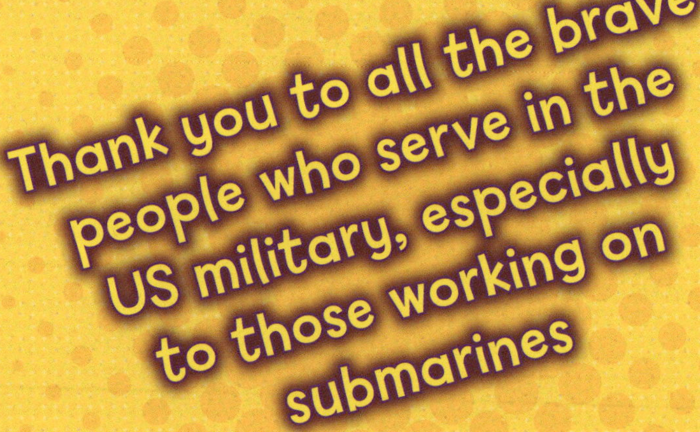

Lerner Publications Company
An imprint of Lerner Publishing Group, Inc.
241 First Avenue North
Minneapolis, MN 55401 USA

For reading levels and more information, look up this title at www.lernerbooks.com.

Main body text set in Billy Infant Regular. Typeface provided by SparkType.

Editor: Cole Nelson **Designer:** Martha Kranes

Library of Congress Cataloging-in-Publication Data

Names: Miller, Marie-Therese, author.
Title: Strong submarines / Marie-Therese Miller.
Description: Minneapolis : Lerner Publications, [2025] | Series: Lightning bolt books : Mighty military vehicles | Includes bibliographical references and index. | Audience: Ages 6–9 | Audience: Grades 2–3 | Summary: "Sometimes ships need to move without being seen. That's when the US Navy uses submarines. Explore the technology and history behind these secret ships beneath the sea"— Provided by publisher.
Identifiers: LCCN 2023039276 (print) | LCCN 2023039277 (ebook) | ISBN 9798765626146 (lib. bdg.) | ISBN 9798765629000 (pbk.) | ISBN 9798765635322 (epub)
Subjects: LCSH: United States. Navy—Submarine forces—Juvenile literature. | Submarines (Ships)—United States—Juvenile literature.
Classification: LCC V858 .M53 2005 (print) | LCC V858 (ebook) | DDC 359.9/30973—dc23/eng/20230922

LC record available at https://lccn.loc.gov/2023039276
LC ebook record available at https://lccn.loc.gov/2023039277

Manufactured in the United States of America
1-1009906-51948-10/26/2023

Table of Contents

US Navy Submarines

A submarine glides on the ocean's surface. A loud alarm sounds. The submarine slips deep below the sea's surface.

Submarines are powerful vessels that sometimes sail at the ocean's surface. Most often they search for enemies deep under the oceans.

Ohio-class submarines are the largest submarines in the US Navy.

They are known as the Silent Service because they are hard to detect. Their missions are secret.

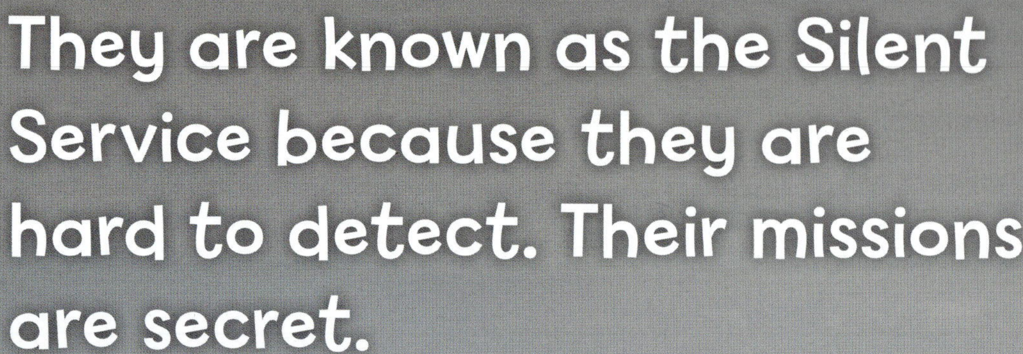

Inside Submarines

US Navy submarines have a control room. From there, the crew steers the submarine and controls how deep it goes.

Most US Navy submarines have periscopes. These long tubes let sailors see what's happening above water when they aren't too deep.

Periscopes use mirrors and lenses to see above the water.

Newer attack submarines have masts with cameras instead of periscopes.

Submarines use sonar to find objects underwater. Sonar works by sending out sound waves. The sound waves bounce back to the submarine when they hit an object.

Navy submarines are powered by nuclear reactors. They need to be refueled after about twenty years. The reactor turns a propeller that moves the submarine.

Sailors need oxygen to breathe when they are underwater. The submarine has a machine that changes water into oxygen and hydrogen.

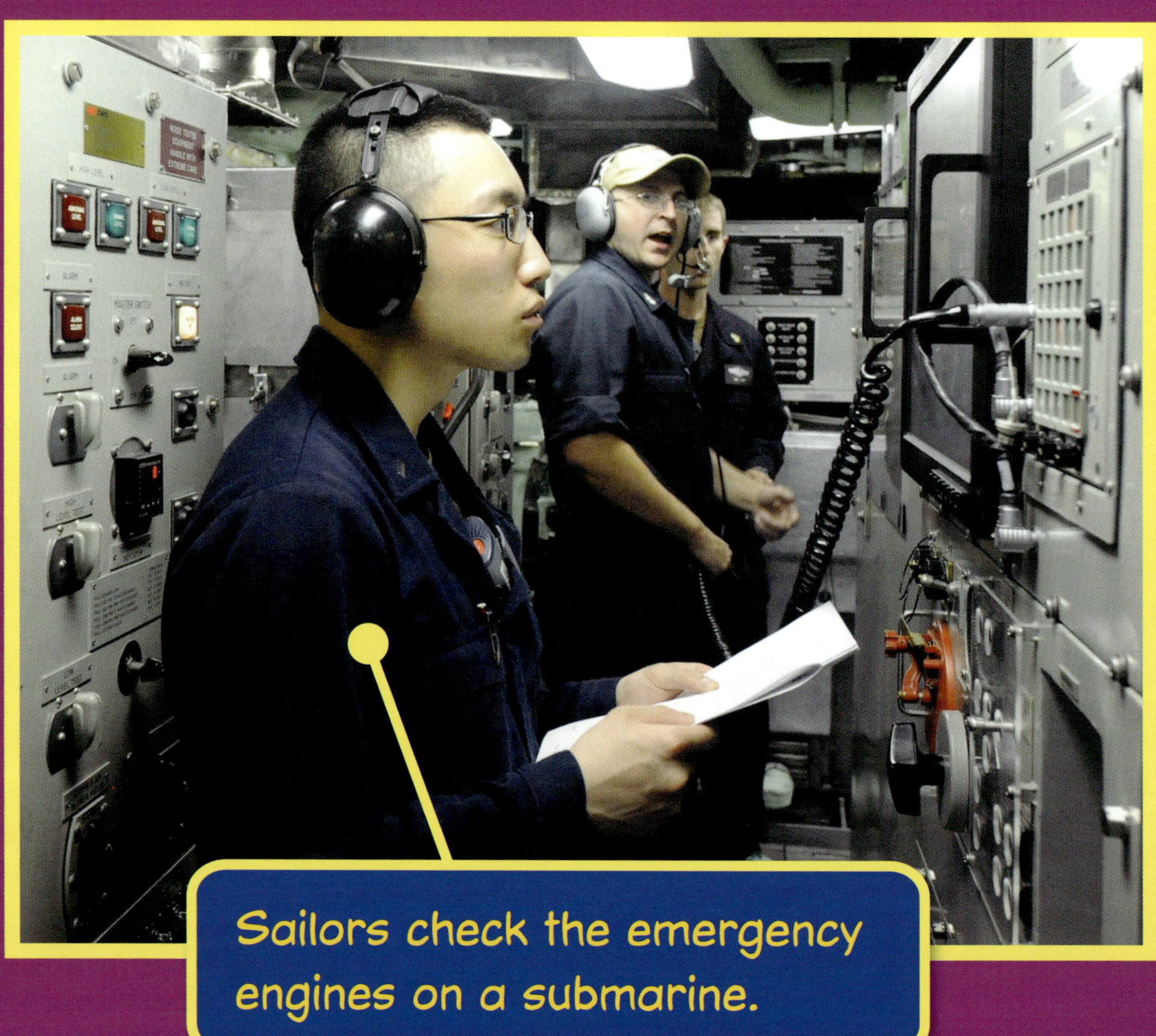

Sailors check the emergency engines on a submarine.

Military submarines hold many weapons. Many submarines have torpedoes on board.

Some submarines carry up to twenty nuclear missiles. These missiles can be launched from the submarine.

Sailors aboard submarines sleep in small areas. Sometimes their sleeping racks are next to the missiles or torpedoes.

Sailors eat their meals on the mess decks. They can play games and watch movies there too.

Sailors relax on board a submarine.

Beneath the Sea

Ohio-class submarines are 560 feet (171 m) long. That's nearly the length of two football fields.

Gold crew sailors practice sailing a submarine.

These submarines have a crew of about 160 sailors. They have two crews, the Blue and the Gold. These crews take turns on the submarine.

The US Navy is building larger submarines that will join the fleet in 2031. Even bigger and better submarines are sure to join them in the future.

Vehicle Diagram

Submarine

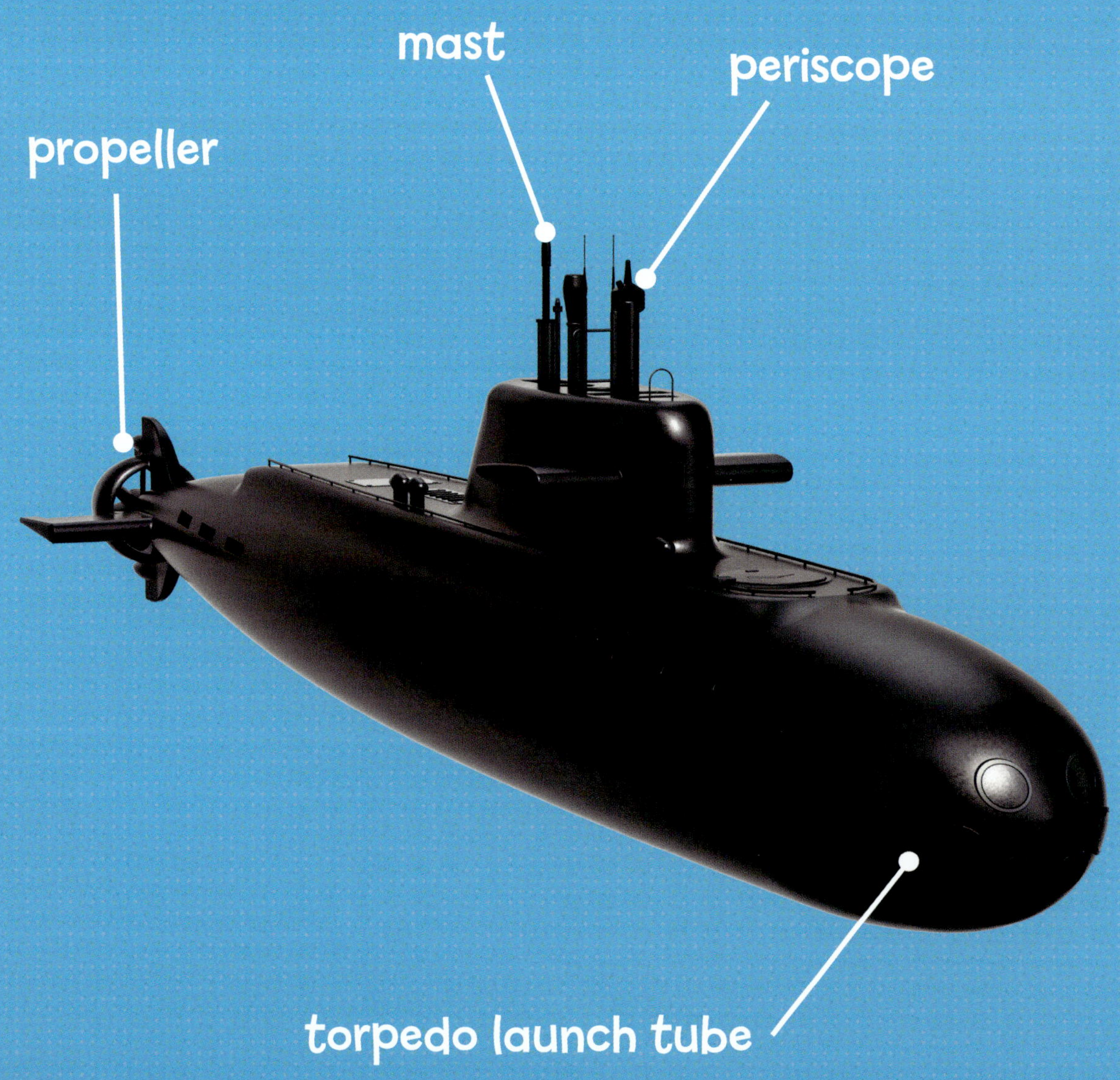

Fun Facts

- Helicopters can bring food and supplies to submarines at sea.

- Ohio-class submarines can spend seventy-seven days at sea.

- Future Columbia-class submarines won't ever have to refuel.

Glossary

detect: to discover the presence of

fleet: a group of ships under a single command

mast: a long pole rising from the deck of a ship

missile: a flying weapon that has its own engine

mission: a specific task

nuclear reactor: a machine that involves changing atoms to create energy

periscope: a tube with prisms, mirrors, or lenses used to show what is out of sight

sound wave: energy released through air or water when an object vibrates

vessel: a watercraft bigger than a rowboat

Learn More

Britannica Kids: Submarine
https://kids.britannica.com/kids/article/submarine
/390261

Kiddle: Submarine Facts for Kids
https://kids.kiddle.co/Submarine

Kiddle: US Navy SEALs Facts for Kids
https://kids.kiddle.co/United_States_Navy_SEALs

Miller, Marie-Therese. *Land and Water Combat Vehicles*. Minneapolis: Lerner Publications, 2025.

Pettiford, Rebecca. *Submarines*. Minneapolis: Bellwether Media, 2022.

Rogers, Marie. *Incredible Submarines*. New York: PowerKids, 2022.

Index

Photo Acknowledgments

Image credits: U.S. Navy/Mass Communication Specialist 2nd Class Jasmine Suarez, p. 4; U.S. Marine Corps/Sgt. Audrey M. C. Rampton, p. 5; U.S. Navy/Mass Communication Specialist 1st Class Ace Rheaume, p. 6; U.S. Navy/Lt. Ed Early, p. 7; U.S. Navy/Mass Communication Specialist 1st Class Amanda R. Gray, pp. 8, 18; Brendan Smialowski/AFP via Getty Images, p. 9; Getty Images, p. 10; U.S. Navy/Lt. Scott Miller, p. 11; U.S. Navy/Chief Mass Communication Specialist Darryl Wood, pp. 12, 15; U.S. Navy/Lieutenant Lauren Spaziano, p. 13; U.S. Navy/Mass Communication Specialist 1st Class Ronald Gutridge, p. 14; Chris Ison/PA Images via Getty Images, p. 16; U.S. Navy/Mass Communication Specialist 2nd Class Aaron Xavier Saldana, p. 17; U.S. Navy/Ashley Cowan, p. 19; AlexLMX/Shutterstock, p.20.

Cover: U.S. Navy, courtesy of General Dynamics Electric Boat.